YOU CAN

take amazing photos

Lillian Spibey

CONTENTS

YOU CAN TAKE AMAZING PHOTOS

Taking amazing photos is really fun!
This book will give you loads of inspiration so that
YOU CAN go and take your own super snaps.

Grab a camera or camera phone, look all around, and
prepare to take some amazing photos! This book is full
of activities that you can do in your own home – inside
or out – and other activities that will take you further
away from home – subjects to photograph can be found
everywhere!

There are activities for everyone – whether you want to
photograph a friend in action at sports day, see the world
from an ant's perspective or get creative with shadows.

There are also plenty of spaces in the book for you to
jot down ideas for new photos, plan a story told by
photos and prepare a photographic treasure hunt.
So what are you waiting for? Read on, and then go
and take amazing photos!

The activities in this book have been tried and tested, and the photographs have been taken by kids your age too!

Before you start snapping, there are a couple things to remember. First, you can hold the camera or phone camera in two ways:

LANDSCAPE

Holding the camera horizontally, or as photographers say 'in the landscape position', is a great way to capture big views and landscapes.

PORTRAIT

Holding the camera vertically or in the 'portrait position' makes it easier to capture tall subjects such as trees and people.

Try to hold the camera or phone camera still when you take a photograph, as this will keep the images sharp and clear.

Each activity in this book will help you to learn more about taking great photos and when you finish, you'll have an amazing set of great images that can be shared with family and friends.

Now turn the page and start taking amazing photos!

ALL ABOUT... CAMERAS

Cameras are amazing pieces of technology! They can have big or small lenses, be brightly coloured and make lots of snapping noises!

Here's how they work...

shutter button

flash

lens

camera body

The lens controls the:

✳ focus (sharpness of the photo)

✳ zoom (gets closer to the subject)

✳ aperture (blurs or sharpens the background)

The camera body holds the:

✳ shutter (controls sharp or blurry action)

✳ sensor (records the image)

The screen or viewfinder is what you look through to see your subject.

The shutter button is what you press to take the photograph.

TIP!

Press the shutter button down halfway to get the focus dot or square to light up, so you know your subject is in focus!

Find the settings or mode dial on the camera, and look for the following settings:

flower   landscape   sports   portrait

Each of these settings is great to use for the activities in the book and will help you take better photographs.

Draw your camera in the space below
and label the:

✸ camera body   ✸ flash   ✸ lens   ✸ shutter button

ALL ABOUT...
PHONE CAMERAS

Phone cameras take great photographs and fit in your pocket.

FOCUS – Tap the screen so a square appears on the subject. Do you notice how your subject is now the sharpest part of the image?

SELF-TIMER – Find the self-timer tool as it is great for taking selfies or if you want to appear in the photograph without holding the camera. Once you turn the self-timer on, you then need to push the shutter button to start the timer, and you will have 10 seconds (or a given amount of time) to get in front of it. Try it!

SHUTTER BUTTON – When pressed, the button opens and closes the shutter to let the light in. Push this button to take a photograph.

FLASH – Look for the flash icon if you need more light in your photograph.

ZOOM – If you want to get closer to your subject, put your thumb and first finger together on the screen and push out. You are now zooming into the photograph!

TIP!

The longer you hold down the shutter button, the more images it will take. Try it!

Look for these settings on a phone's camera and try them out yourself.

Answer these questions about phone cameras.

1 When you use the flash, what happens?

_____

_____

2 If you hold down the shutter button and count to five, what happens?

_____

_____

3 Once you've turned on the self-timer, how many seconds do you have until the phone takes a photograph?

_____

_____

4 Place a toy in front of the camera and tap the focus square on something behind the toy or in the background. What happens?

_____

_____

5 Find something small to photograph. How can you get closer?

_____

_____

9

FOCUS

When you find the perfect image, the last thing you want is a fuzzy photograph. Using the focus is super important and helps to create sharply focused images.

BLURRY OR FOCUSED?

Can you tell which images are out of focus and blurry, and which images are focused and sharp? Write 'focused' or 'blurry' next to each photo and draw a green square around the sharpest part of the image, if there is one!

Tilly

Sophie

Jemima

Answers: blurry, focused, focused

How to focus

WITH A CAMERA: inside the viewfinder or screen, some cameras have black and red focus dots and others have green squares.

1 Look through the viewfinder, or on the screen, and push the shutter button halfway down.

2 You should see the green square or black/red dot appear. Put it on your subject and take the photo.

WITH A PHONE: make sure you tap the focus square on your screen to be on the most important part of your photograph. Doing this will make that part the sharpest, most focused bit of your image.

The red dot is on the centre of the flower.

See the green square?

Look at these photos of the pigeons and Houses of Parliament. Can you see how Ellie has moved her focus and changed the look of the photo?

LIGHT

Light is all around you. Do you notice how the colour of the light changes with the seasons? Or how on cloudy days the light looks grey? Sunsets make the light look soft and warm, and on sunny days the light can look strong and bright.

Think about where you put your light in your photograph to make it pop! Try having the sun behind you like a spotlight, or use the strong rays of sunlight to sidelight (light up from the side) your subject, adding shadows and texture.

Louis has captured the sun painting the tops of the leaves with light.

Mimi looked at the floor and photographed the light from a window. It's created a cool spotlight!

There are so many ways you can use light creatively in your photographs. Whizzing Ferris wheels, candles and fairy lights are great examples of lights to capture.

What kind of light is used in these photos?

(Hint: candles, torches, sunlight, light bulbs, fairy lights…)

William

Candles

Alex

Light bulbs/Fairy lights

Bella

Sunlight

WHO ARE YOU?

Photographs are a wonderful way to show your friends and family details about yourself and share ideas. You can photograph your favourite clothes, take silly selfies and even take a photograph of your room.

Start by thinking about who you are.
What are your favourite things?

⭐ Do you like to go out on walks? If so, photograph your shoes!

⭐ Do you like to play sport? Photograph some sports equipment.

⭐ Do you like to hang out with friends? Photograph your friends!

Can you see how Emese has put both of her bright red shoes together to capture the shoes in one photo?

Millie likes the sky and found a beautiful reflection of it in a puddle. Look in puddles next time you want to photograph the sky!

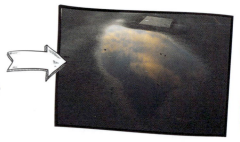

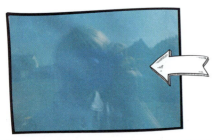

Isaac took a cool selfie using the reflection he found in a window that had a blue curtain. Can you find your reflection in a window or mirror at home?

Write ten GREAT things about yourself, and then go out and take those photos!

1. I Love hanging out with my friends.
2. I love climbing trees and
3. I love designing my outfit for the day
4. I love to play sport.
5. My favourite colour is blue.
6. I love any breed of dog.
7. I love going sledging and playing in the snow.
8. I love decorating my tree of house for Christmas.
9. I love going on boats over waves
10. I like going to the beach on holiday.

COLOUR

How many colours can you see around you? There are so many colours and the more you look, the more you will see! Choosing a colour to photograph on its own is a great way to show off detail.

Look at the colours below and write down ideas on where you could photograph them.

The green grass & leaves at a park.

Red flowers or strawberrys.

A picture of yellow heath trees or the sun.

The sky with birds in new.

A virbena plant.

The trees at Hampsted Heath.

A picture of the night sky.

Starting off inside, look for colourful pens, blankets or even food! Choose a colour and fill the camera's screen or viewfinder with it. Make sure your image is sharply focused and that you aren't too close.

The blue sky is a colourful subject and William added a bright yellow ball in his photo. Do you think William threw the ball and snapped the photo himself, or asked a friend to help?

Hatty noticed that a tree's leaves in her local park had turned golden yellow for autumn. Instead of just photographing a yellow leaf, she took a photograph of all the leaves on the tree.

Charlotte found some cut-up tomatoes, piled them up in a bowl next to a window and filled the camera frame with the colour red! Is this photo about tomatoes or the colour red?

ACTION

Lights, camera, action! When you take a photograph of a moving person or object, you capture the movement in a single shot. It's a great way to show action and have some fun too!

When photographing action on a camera, look to see if there is an action or sports setting:

Using this setting makes the camera's shutter open and close quickly to stop the action and capture the movement sharply.

Timing is a big part of taking great action photographs. Start taking photographs a second or two before the action begins, or tell your friend to jump on 3 (as in 1, 2, 3!) and you start taking photos on 2!

Sam captured his friend playing basketball. Look how he was able to photograph the ball in the air!

Try getting low to make your friends' jumps look BIG, like Amelia!

Hold the shutter button down for 5–10 seconds, to take a lot of photographs. This helps you capture all of the action! Check out the photos of Elliot jumping!

Try and photograph all the actions listed below.

* ball in the air
* running
* spinning
* dancing
* leaves in the air

water running

jumping

hair flicks

Remember to hold the shutter down for 5 seconds and to count 1, 2, 3!

BE AN ANT!

Try being an ANT for the day – this means you have to take photographs wherever an ANT can crawl! Photographs are more interesting when they are taken from a different viewpoint or not from eye level. You can make the world look like such a different place!

The more you can make everyday life look different, the more eye catching and interesting your photograph will be. Hold the camera up, down, right and left. Try taking photographs indoors along the floor, looking up a wall and along a counter. If you pretend the camera is an ant, your photographs will make the world around you look new!

Try putting a camera at the base of a tree, like Gabriella! It looks like a giant!

Dandan put her camera directly in the grass, making it look like a jungle!

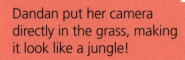

Look for bright colours and get close! Or place the camera on a railing, just like an ant would crawl along it! Think outside the box. Remember, ants crawl up as well as down!

When you change your perspective or camera angle, it changes the way the world looks. Have a look at the images below and write where the camera was when the photo was taken.

Where is the camera?

TIP!

If you have a camera, use the flower or close-up 🌷 setting for taking ant photos.

Lily-Rose

Rupert

Mabel

THE RULE OF THIRDS

The Rule of Thirds is a great way to help you plan your photographs. When you look through the viewfinder on the camera or the screen on a phone, imagine a noughts and crosses board. Try to place your subject where the lines meet.

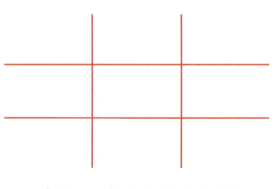

Can you see how Wesley's flower is at the top of the frame? He's also turned his camera upside down!

If you like taking photographs of landscapes or big views, think about where you place the horizon. The horizon is where the ground meets the sky. Try to place the horizon on the bottom or the top line of the noughts and crosses board.

TIP!

Try not to put the horizon in the middle of the photograph.

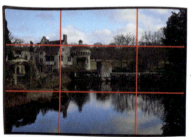

Hollie has placed the horizon on the top line of the noughts and crosses board.

Draw the noughts and crosses boards on the photos!

Siarrah

Oscar

Macie

Using the Rule of Thirds can be as simple as not putting your subject in the middle of the photograph. Give it a go and see how it changes how your photograph looks!

LOOKING FOR LINES

Lines run up, down, right, left and diagonal! Lines are great to photograph as they lead the viewer's eye through the image. It's like using an arrow to point where you want everyone to look.

Chloe has captured the lines in a leaf. Do you see how the lines lead you to the middle of the leaf?

Where has Isaac placed his camera in this photo? He's really used the lines creatively.

The circular lines create a pattern, and frame the yellow centre. What do you think Sebastian has photographed?

Remember that lines are your subject, so get as close as you can to frame them with a camera.

Draw all the lines that are used in each photo in the rectangles.

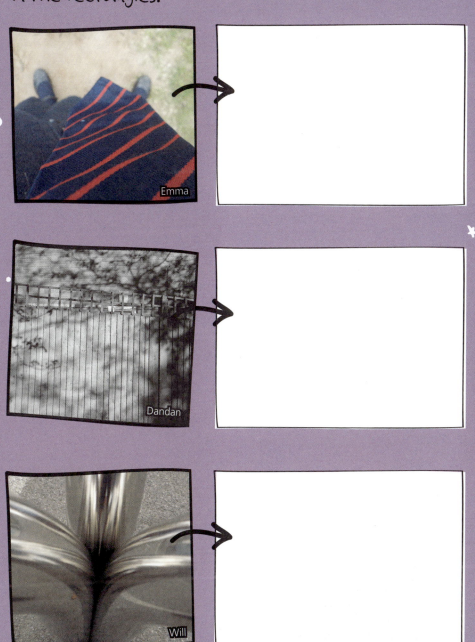

Emma

Dandan

Will

25

GET CLOSE

Try getting close and taking photographs of the small objects around you. Taking close-up or macro photographs is a way to make small items look big. Show off the detail of your favourite button, or capture the petals of the flowers in your local park.

What is it? Guess what our photographers have photographed by getting CLOSE to their subjects!

Ronit

Alma

Molly

Answers: tree seed, pinwheel, dog's nose

The trick is making sure that you aren't TOO CLOSE, and you still have the camera or phone's focusing square on your subject.

 If you are using a camera, look to see if there is a flower or close-up setting. This will help the camera focus closely on your subject.

If you are using a phone, just make sure you've tapped the focus square on your subject and it looks clear, not fuzzy.

TIP!

First, use your feet to get closer to your subject, and then the zoom. Your photos will always look better if you get closer with your feet!

Emma has put her camera close to the middle of the flower, framing the circle, and using her camera's focus.

Zeph got low and physically close to the leaf. What are those red dots?

Now go out and get close to your subjects!

BUGS

Photographing bugs is fun! You can start with the slow movers such as slugs and snails, and then move onto the quicker moving bugs such as bees, woodlice and butterflies.

⚡For slower moving bugs such as slugs and snails, you might need to use your flash if you find them in the shade, or under a tree or rock.

When you take photographs of the faster moving insects such as butterflies, bees and dragonflies, you'll need to be quick to capture them in your images. Try using your zoom to get closer so you don't disturb them.

TIP!

When taking a photo of a moving bug, hold the shutter button down for at least 5 seconds so that the camera or phone takes many photographs.

Jake put his camera in front of the snail, and caught it on the move!

Jack captured this grayling butterfly using the action setting on his camera. The butterfly is super sharp as a result.

The action setting on a camera is great to use to capture bugs. This setting makes sure the shutter is opening and closing quickly to capture the bug's movement.

After you've taken your photos, you can find out what each type of bug is and label the photo.

Name that bug!

Sam

Martin

Isaac

Answers: Harlequin ladybird larva, snail, grasshopper

USE SHADOWS

Shadows are everywhere and make great subjects for photographs. Photographing a shadow is a fun way to make the world around you look different. Everything can create an interesting shadow; it just depends on the time of day you look for it.

Have you tried photographing the shadow of everyday things such as lamp posts, bicycles, or even your dog? If you only take a photograph of the shadow and leave out what is casting the shadow, your photo becomes more interesting, like a guessing game!

Try taking a photo of your shadow in the air! Can you get both feet off the ground like Elliot?

Find fences or a window to frame your shadow, like Eleanor.

Do you see how Eleanor and Elliot have held their cameras in these photos? Try holding a camera vertically so you can capture the length of your shadow.

Taking photos when the sun is lower in the sky, such as early morning or late afternoon, will make the shadows appear longer and more abstract. Try to go for a walk at these times to see how many different shadows you can capture.

Shadows can also create fun stories. What do you think is happening in the photos below?

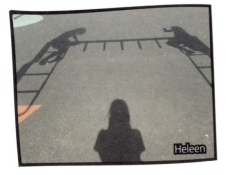
Heleen

Eleanor

Gabriella

Now go out and make your own story with the shadows around you!

PATTERNS

A pattern is a design or shape that repeats itself. Photographing patterns is a fun way to capture the world. Can you see any patterns around you? Check out your floor or window – do you see repeating lines or shapes?

Think about how you want to capture your patterns. You can take the photograph from above, or try setting a camera on the pattern itself.

Buildings, cars and trees in a row can also make a pattern – you don't only have to photograph the little things.

TIP!

Check out your clothes and hair! You can find great patterns there too.

Ellie captured a yellow and orange pattern. Where do you think the pattern was?

Niamh climbed under some playground equipment and photographed looking up!

Looking for patterns will help develop your eye for a good photograph and you'll start to find them everywhere you look. Draw these patterns.

Window with 4 rectangles of glass	Wooden fence
5 apples	Piano keys
Braided piece of hair	Staircase

FRAME WITHIN A FRAME

When you look through a viewfinder or screen, you are always framing your subject. It's helpful to frame your subject so everyone knows what to look at in the photograph.

To add more fun to your photographs, try photographing through another frame, such as a hole in the fence, a window, or even through some branches.

Erin put her camera on one end of a cone and pointed the open end at her friend's feet. Look at her frame, it's red!

Rosie framed the playground with the tree branches.

There are many frames around you – if you go to your local playground, try photographing through the square netting on a football goal, or through one of the climbing frame doorways or tubes.

As a starting point, cut a frame out of a sheet of paper, and hold it in front of the camera to frame your subjects.

TIP!

Make sure your focus square or dot is on your subject, not the frame.

Can you find the frames and then circle them in these photographs?

Akash

Harry

HOME

Photographing your home is a great way to capture your daily life. Everyone lives differently, and with cameras, you can show your friends and family your daily life and how you live it.

Think about your favourite place to sit or where you like to eat your breakfast, and then go and photograph it! You get to choose how to take the photograph. Do you hold the camera above your breakfast, like a giant looking down at it? Or do you place the camera on the table like an ant, looking straight at your breakfast?

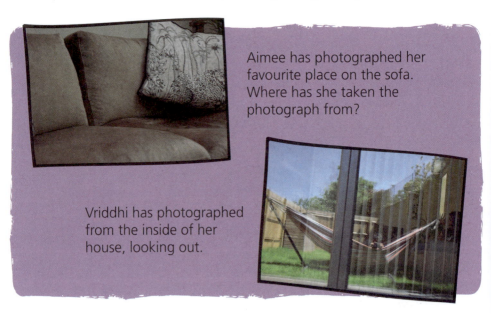

Aimee has photographed her favourite place on the sofa. Where has she taken the photograph from?

Vriddhi has photographed from the inside of her house, looking out.

Taking photographs of your own home and what it means to you makes the photos special and one of a kind. Share the photographs with your friends and family to celebrate your idea of home.

List your 5 favourite things about your home and then photograph them!

1 _____

2 _____

3 _____

4 _____

5 _____

Here are some ideas...

Luke

TIP!

⚡ Use your flash if you are in a dark room, or wait and photograph the room when it's lit by sunshine.

Ishan

Jaime

TEXTURE

Texture is the way an object feels or looks – it can be soft, rough, smooth, and so on. Everything you see has a texture.

Find something to photograph that is...

* soft
* smooth
* hard

* prickly
* wet
* dry

* shiny
* dull
* squishy

Anna

Sophie

Bea

Look around. Can you see a window? How would you describe a window's texture? Perhaps shiny or smooth. How can you capture the shine of the window? Try using your flash, as it will make the window appear shiny!

Think about filling the frame with a texture, so that's all you can see. Can you see how both these photographers have filled their frames with textures?

Johnny has filled the frame with smooth rocks. How close do you think his camera was to the rocks?

Fergus captured the sharpness of the Teasel plant. Ouch! It looks sharp!

TIP!

Remember to make sure the camera's focusing dot or square is on the texture, so your photograph is super sharp!

Now go out and photograph some textures!

BLACK & WHITE

What do you think when you see a black and white photograph? Do you think it looks old? Or perhaps it looks dramatic? The first ever photograph was taken in 1826, and the image was in black and white.

Photographing in black and white is a great way to show off the details in a photograph. Without the colour, there are fewer distractions.

When photographs are taken in black and white, sometimes it takes longer to understand the photograph. Has Heleen photographed a claw or a branch? You decide!

Black and white images are timeless, often making the viewer think more about when they were taken. Can you find the black and white setting on a camera and take some photographs that look old?

TIP!

You can change the colour of your image to black and white after you've taken it.

Circle the image you like better.
Colour, or black and white?

TELL A STORY

Telling a story can be done in one photograph or many! Photography is a creative way to tell a story, but you need to plan out your story, and think about the photographs before you start snapping!

Sophie has photographed a mystery. Can you guess it? Hint: look at the boy's feet!

If you are going to take one photograph, include as many details as you can about your subject, and think about where everything is placed.

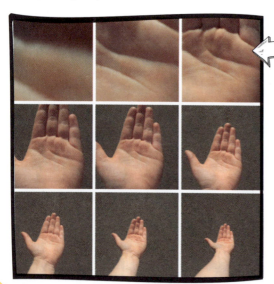

Jake has photographed his hand moving away from the camera in nine shots – simple and fun!

TIP!

Try printing out your images to make a flip book of your story!

Story planning board

If you are going to take more than one photo to tell a story, first plan it out. Get a piece of paper and draw however many frames you need for the story. Try six to start. Then write or draw what will happen in each photo. This way you won't miss a shot!

Story ideas

* flowers (perhaps they lose their petals?)
* an apple (maybe it gets eaten – yum!)
* your friend (running and jumping)

Now plan your own here.

PORTRAITS

Photographing people can help us learn more about them. Taking their portrait, or a photograph that shows their head and shoulders, is a way to show off their amazing smile, happy laugh or bright eyes.

If you are using a camera, look for the portrait setting as this will help to blur the background behind your subject and will often turn the flash on.

The person in the photo doesn't always have to be looking at the camera. Amelia was captured climbing a tree!

Sam used the black and white setting, putting the focus on his expression – SMILE!

TIP!

Try holding the camera vertically so the photograph frames your subject well.

Match the emotions to the portrait.

Happy

Surprised

Silly

Now ask your friends and family if you can take their portrait! You could print the image out and give it to them as a gift.

HIDE AND SEEK

Have you ever played 'hide and seek' with a camera before? Ask a friend to help, or you can use the self-timer and hide yourself!

1 Look for a hiding place (indoors or outdoors).

2 Ask your friend to hide there (or you do it) but make sure you can still see a bit of their foot or head; they can't be completely hidden.

3 Take the photograph!

Erin tilted her camera up, which hid all of her friend, except for his hand!

Can you spot James' friend? James has used a lot of layers to hide his friend... keep looking!

TIP!

Try photographing in black and white to make it even harder to find the person hiding!

Playing camera hide and seek is a fun game! Get creative with the small details you can see through the camera, and try to make it harder to spot them with each photograph!

Can you find the people hiding in the photos? Circle them when you do!

Florence

Eliana

Isaac

WHAT SEASON IS IT?

Winter, spring, summer and autumn are great to capture with a camera. What season is it right now? Try and capture the best parts of the current season!

Ellie has captured the colour of the autumn leaves, by holding the branch up against the blue sky. What a lovely autumn day!

Looking for the details for each season is a great way to start.

⭐ **WINTER** – Can you show how cold it is! Capture the ice, snow and frosty mornings!

⭐ **SPRING** – Can you show the growth of a flower or plant? Capture the bud and then photograph it as it opens or grows!

⭐ **SUMMER** – Can you show how warm it is? Capture a pet playing in the water, or a friend playing an outdoor sport.

⭐ **AUTUMN** – Can you capture the leaves changing colour? Find a tree and photograph it daily as it changes from green to gold to brown.

Evie photographed the pom pom on her friend's winter hat. It's a great representation of winter!

Write the season next to each photo.

Eleanor.

Skylar

Archie

49

SELFIES

Selfies, or self-portraits, are a popular way to take a photograph of yourself. The more smiles, laughter and fun you can show in the photo, the better! Let's explore the different ways you can take a great selfie!

The first technique is to hold the camera at an arm's length from your face. Turn the camera so the lens is facing you, and make sure you have your finger on the shutter button. Try to photograph as many different emotions as you can: happy, sad, hungry, tired, angry and silly!

Anton has taken a photograph of himself – but he's upside down… how's he done that?

TIP!

Your selfie does not always have to include your face. Try taking a photograph of your feet and then another photo of your hands.

Next, try turning on your self-timer so you can be hands free! This way you can run, jump and twirl in front of the camera and show more about you!

Oli has set his camera up on a picnic table, turned on self-timer, and jumped HIGH! What a great expression and jump!

TIP!

Try to get the timing right. The camera will usually give you 10 seconds to get ready!

CAPTURE YOUR SELF-PORTRAIT!

Photograph:

- your eyes
- your face
- your knees
- a jump
- a twirl
- your thumb
- your smile
- your feet
- your hair
- your whole body

TREES

Photographing trees is easy – they don't move unless it's really windy!

First, try to take a photograph of the whole tree. You might need to be quite far away from the tree to include the top and bottom in the photograph. Hold the camera in portrait position (vertically) too!

Next, try to capture the details on the tree such as the leaves, bark and branches. Remember to get close or use the zoom to make the detail the biggest part of the photograph.

Can you see how Ellie has framed the trees in the centre of the image? Great layering!

A tree's colours, leaves and overall shape change throughout the seasons. Try to take photographs of the same tree throughout the year to see how it changes.

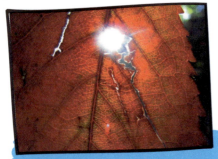

Ben found a red leaf and captured the sunshine peeking through it.

TIP!

If you are using a camera, look for the landscape setting so the whole tree is sharply focused.

More ideas on how to photograph trees...

Theo

Oscar

Draw a tree and label all the different things you can photograph!

5 SENSES

Sight, smell, hearing, taste and touch are the 5 senses. We use them all the time to help us understand the world around us. Can you name which body part you use for each sense?

Match the sense to the body part.

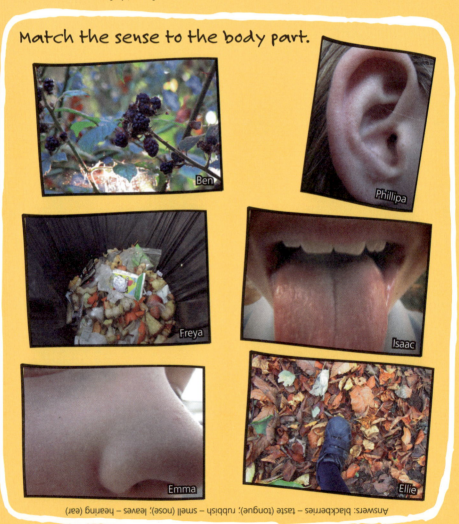

Ben

Phillipa

Freya

Isaac

Emma

Ellie

Answers: blackberries – taste (tongue); rubbish – smell (nose); leaves – hearing (ear)

What could you photograph to represent each of the 5 senses?

Think about what you can see, what you can touch, what smells good, what makes a noise and what tastes amazing! Then go out and take those photographs!

Have you ever smelled lavender? Phillipa photographed the purple lavender to remind her of the flower's amazing scent.

Martha photographed her friend's eye to represent sight.

What is your favourite sense? Do you like the smell of food? If so, take some creative photographs of food when you are next in the kitchen or at a bakery. If you like the sense of sight, take a photograph of what you like to look at, such as a view out of the window.

ALPHABET

Eloise, Erin and Thomasina photographed an object that looks like a letter and then something that starts with the same letter. Can you name the letters and the objects?

Eloise

Letter: _____

Object: _____

Erin

Letter: _____

Object: _____

Thomasina

Letter: _____

Object: _____

Letters can be found anywhere! They don't have to be perfect – as long as the letters are recognisable, take the picture! Challenge your eye to look and find letters everywhere.

Think about the letter 'T'. It has two parts, and can be found on a window, floor tile, or brick – do you see it? Photograph it!

Rupert saw a bench, turned his camera vertically, and made it into an 'E'.

Get creative with how you hold the camera to frame the letters. Think big, as you can also use buildings, street lamps and bridges to make letters.

Edward has made a lowercase 'i' – do you see it? The clock is the dot of the 'i' and the student's body is the line of the 'i'.

TIP!

Try to keep the backgrounds around your letters simple, making the letters easy to spot.

Once you've photographed the whole alphabet, you can make great gifts! Print out each letter to spell a name or greeting, and then make a cool card or poster.

STILL LIFE

Have you ever taken a photograph of an onion? Or how about a rock or a shell? Photographing natural objects or taking still-life photographs draws attention to the amazing details that we often miss.

To take a still-life photograph, you need to set up a small studio.

First, you'll need a backdrop. Either use two sheets of black paper: one for under the object and one for behind, or black fabric like a sweatshirt or sheet.

Second, you'll need light. Set up your studio near a window or in a brightly lit room. Now find your object!

Poppy photographed a pear, and really captured its shape. The pear stands out against the black background. Do you think it tastes as nice as it looks?

Saskia stood above her studio and photographed downwards, using her flash. What's going on with that vegetable – do you think it's real?

Get creative and cut the fruit or vegetables in half to show what's inside! Taking the photo in your studio will produce a great looking, professional image. Who needs to know it's just a couple of pieces of paper and a carrot?

Can you guess what's been photographed in these still-life photos? After you've guessed, take your own!

TIP!

⚡ Turn on your flash if you need more light in your photograph.

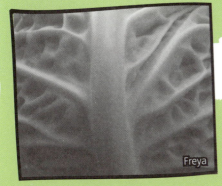

Freya

Georgina

Lucy

Answers: cabbage, strawberry, banana

SHAPES

What do these all have in common?

They are shapes! Shapes make up structures, such as houses, buildings and even this book!

Look for a rectangle... for example a TV, phone or an oven window. Can you frame the rectangle in the camera's viewfinder? Make sure to get all 4 sides in the photograph. Take the photo and you have captured your first shape!

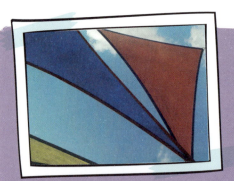

Nancy found some triangles and captured them against the bright blue sky.

Livia has used the circles as frames in her photograph. What do you think Livia has held in front of her camera that has lots of circles?

Once you've started spotting all the shapes around you, get creative with how you use them in your photographs. Think about photographing through them, or use them to frame your subject.

Name the shapes that you can see in these photos.

Ella

Caera

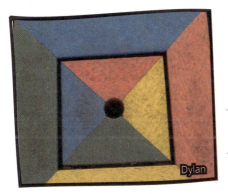
Dylan

DRAW WITH LIGHT

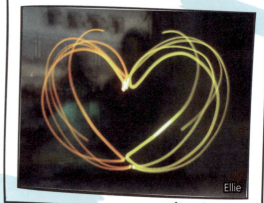
Ellie

Have you ever drawn with a torch before? It's fun and easy to do.

Think about what you'd like to draw, and practise with the torch before you start taking photos. It might take a couple of tries to get the photograph you imagined, so keep trying!

Here is what you need:

1 A dark room, or wait until it's completely dark outside.

2 A torch or mobile phone light.

3 The phone or camera's self-timer, or a friend to take the photograph.

4 For a camera, look for the firework setting, or use a 10-second shutter speed. For a mobile phone, download a slow shutter speed app, and use 10 seconds or more!

Now stand in front of the camera, point your torch towards the camera, and draw with light!

Martha has multiplied herself! Turn the torch on yourself for 1 second and then turn it off. Take a step and repeat.

Harrison used a red plastic wrapper over his torch, and made the colour of the light red!

Ask a friend to shine a torch on their face for 1 second and then draw with light around them, like Isabella has done.

Try writing 'Hi' or drawing a happy face, like Eve.

TIP!

Put the camera on a desk or table to keep the image sharp and avoid camera shake, or use a tripod.

REFLECTIONS

What do all three photographs have in common?

Reflections! Photographing reflections is a creative way to add layers to your images and can often lead to a guessing game about what is in a photo.

What is being reflected?

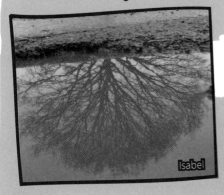

Isabel

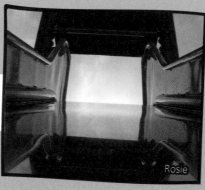

Rosie

Layla

Try taking a photograph of just a reflection, looking at the details created by the reflection. Consider using black and white if there are distracting colours.

Abigail captured her camera's reflection amongst the flowers. Are the flowers inside the window or near the camera?

If you have a small mirror, take it outside and frame different objects in the mirror itself.

TIP!

Make sure your focus dot or square is on the mirror.

Oscar held the mirror up so it reflected the sky. He then took a photograph of the sky in his hand!

See how many reflections you can spot when you go out for a walk. Anything shiny or metallic should give you a reflection, and the more abstract it is, the more interesting the photo!

Find your reflection in a:

 car bonnet   puddle   window

Make sure you photograph these reflections too!

FLASH

Using light is key to being a good photographer. The flash is a bright burst of light that will brighten up whatever is in front of the camera.

⚡ Find it on a camera or phone and turn it on.

Using the flash brightens your photograph if you are in the shade or indoors.

Anton used the flash to make the leaves in the foreground (front of the photograph) look bright, leaving the background dark. This gives his photograph a spooky effect.

Anton

Simon

Simon photographed some mushrooms under the shade of a tree. Because he used the flash, the mushrooms are brightly lit, and we can see the details.

Livia photographed the donkey on a grey day and turned the flash on in order to capture the movement of its mouth.

Livia

Draw a flash symbol ⚡ next to the photographs where the flash was used.

Jemima

Dan

Edward

TOYS

Gather up your favourite toys for some fun photographs!

Ruby

Edward set his toy dinosaur close to the camera and then ran 3 metres behind it and looked up! His actions make the dinosaur look big. Great use of perspective!

In this photo, Ruby is giving us the impression that the toys are looking out at a view, spending time together. It's a wonderful way to tell a story through a single image.

Edward

TIP!

Try using the self-timer if you'd like to take some interesting perspective photographs like Edward. The self-timer will allow you to appear in the photograph and take the photo.

Make a list of what your favourite toy would like to do. Then go out and photograph your toy doing them!

My toy's name: _____

What my toy would like to do:

1 _____

2 _____

3 _____

4 _____

5 _____

Does your toy like to swim?

Does your toy fly?

Harrison

Sammy

Does your toy take photos?!

Harrison

BLUR

Blur is a creative way to make the world around you appear differently. When using the blurring methods below, your photographs are always going to be a surprise.

BLURRING METHODS

1 VERTICAL BLUR – Move the camera up and down quickly while taking the photograph. Try taking several photographs at a time before viewing the images.

Akash took this photograph of a tree in autumn. As he moved the camera up and down while taking the photo, the final image looks more like a painting than a photograph.

2 WHIRLPOOL BLUR – Find a tree or tall structure to stand under, and point the camera upwards. First, look around to make sure there is nothing you can trip over. Then push the shutter button and spin around in a circle.

Ava found a big tree to spin underneath, and created a cool whirlpool effect.

3 **BLURRY SELFIE –** Turn the camera around to face you, and hold it with two hands. Check the ground to make sure there is nothing to trip on. Spin around in a circle, look at the camera and take the photograph! You could try turning the flash on if you need more light on your face.

Ben captured himself spinning around in the woods, blurring the background with his spins!

TIP!

Use the camera's auto setting to create blurry images. The blurring methods will also work well on a phone.

Can you...

⭐ move the camera left to right, back and forward really quickly?

⭐ move the camera up and down, up and down, up and down?

⭐ spin in a circle with the camera pointing outwards?

⭐ take a selfie with the flash while you spin?

Try your own blurring method – what can you create?

WATER

There are so many ways to photograph water! If you live near the ocean you can capture the waves, or if it's been raining, photograph your feet splashing around in a puddle! Try turning on a tap and photographing the water as it hits the bottom of the sink.

Sam

Sam asked a friend to pop a water balloon on a bench. He was able to capture the moment when the balloon burst!

Zoe

Zoe's friend filled a cup with water, and threw the water outwards. It looks like ice!

Start taking photographs before the action, and continue to hold the shutter button down so you can capture it as it happens.

TIP!

If you are using a camera, turn on the sports or action setting, which will help capture the water. If you are using a phone, hold the shutter button down for 5 seconds, and you'll be able to take a lot of photographs at once.

Bea

Bea turned on a tap, got low and photographed the water as it gathered around the drain.

Can you capture water by:

✴ splashing in a puddle?

✴ turning on a hose pipe?

✴ filling up a plastic water bottle and then squeezing it?

TIP!

Make sure you keep the camera dry!

Nancy

Tegan

LANDSCAPES

What do you think of when you read the word 'landscape'?

Do you think of big skies? Or amazing views?

Capturing big views is a great way to remember family trips, a day out, or the area where you live.

Sophia used the Rule of Thirds, giving the sky more space than the ground. She also framed the image with trees on both sides of the photograph. This helps to push your eye into the middle of the image.

Dulcie held her camera in portrait position (vertically) to capture the frame created by the trees. Natural frames are used by landscape photographers and you can use them too!

Take landscape
photographs:

- ✹ using the Rule of Thirds
  (see pages 22–23)

- ✹ holding the
  camera vertically

- ✹ at sunset

- ✹ using the black and
  white setting

(see pages 22–23)

TIP!

Landscape photographs
look best if you can
take them at the
beginning or end of the
day. The sun's colour
becomes golden and
the shadows are long,
which adds to the
amazing view!

Draw a landscape that is familiar to you.

PETS

Photographing a pet is a fun challenge. Pets move around, and often will not follow many commands, so learning more photographic skills will help you to take great shots.

Try to get close to your pet, using your zoom. Lily has framed her cat's eye, placing it at the top of the photo.

Lily sat on the ground, and was able to take the photograph at the dog's eye level. Changing your perspective is a great way to make your photographs more interesting. Can you see the dog is smiling?

TIP!

Turn on the action setting when photographing pets, as you never know when they are going to move.

If you don't have a pet, you could take a photo of someone else's pet. Don't forget to ask a pet's owner first if you can take the pet's photograph.

Write your pet's name and what you like about them below. If you don't have a pet, think about a pet you know or your dream pet!

Pet's name

_____

My pet is amazing because:

1 _____

_____

_____

_____

2 _____

_____

_____

_____

3 _____

_____

_____

Draw your pet here!

Now try to put the reasons you like your pet into photographs! Have fun!

3 PART PHOTOS

These objects have been photographed in 3 parts and then the photos have been mixed up. Can you put them in the correct order? Label the order of the photos.

Ollie

Lauren

Emma

Do you think you can split your favourite toy or view into three photographs? You can, and a bit of planning will make it even easier.

1 First, find what you want to photograph.

2 Look at the object (or view) through a phone or camera and think about how to split it into three pieces.

3 Take the 3 photographs, trying to make the ends of each photograph meet.

Cici

TIP!

Try standing at least 2 arm's lengths from your subject to make sure you can split it into 3 images.

William photographed his friend Sammy in three parts, and it's great how he captured Sammy taking photos too!

Don't worry too much if the ends of your photographs don't completely match up – it makes the overall image look more abstract and one of a kind. Concentrate on finding different places or objects to split up, and even try splitting them into 2 photos or 4!

FINDING FACES

What do these photographs have in common?

Tillie

Evie

Archie

Answer: Each image has a face in it – can you spot it?

Look for faces around you! Look at light switches, as many have two screws on each side of the switch, making two eyes and a nose. Or look at a plug socket and turn the camera upside down. Can you now see two eyes and a nose?

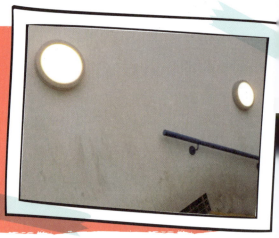

Eloise photographed two lights and a railing – do you see how she's tilted her camera to make the face?

Holding a camera in different positions can help to make the photo look better. Can you figure out how the photographers have held their cameras for the photos above?

Find and circle the face in each photo.

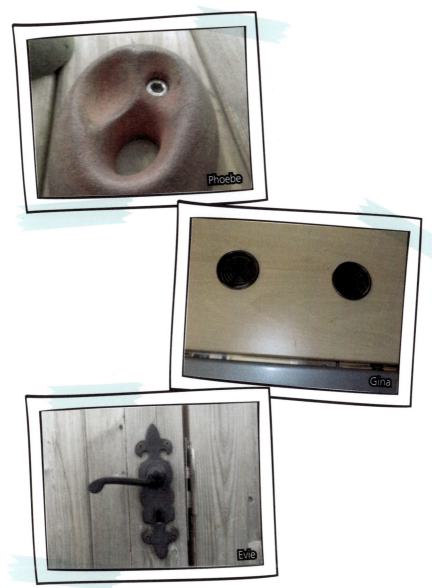

Phoebe

Gina

Evie

Go for a walk around your home and see how many faces you can spot and photograph!

SUNSETS

Photographing the sun as it's setting in the sky is a great way to capture views and landscapes. The sky fills with colours and the buildings or trees are silhouetted or darkened by the bright light of the sun. It's a wonderful part of nature that happens every day.

To capture it through your lens, first think of a place with an open view, such as a local park.

Erica used the Rule of Thirds. She put the horizon at the bottom of the image, making the sky the subject of the photograph.

When you place an object, building or person in front of a sunset, they will become darker or silhouetted as the sky is the brightest part of the image. Think of the silhouettes as an added bonus in front of the colourful sky.

TIP!

After the sun has set, try waiting another 20 minutes to capture the 'blue hour' when the sun has set below the horizon.

Evie photographed a tree against the colourful sky, silhouetting it with the bright light from the sun. The soft colours of the sunset complement the wiry tree branches.

Luca pointed the camera up at the sky and captured the birds in flight. He hasn't included any buildings and trees, making the photograph look very dreamy and colourful.

Capture your own sunset!

⭐ Try using the Rule of Thirds to create layers in your sunset (remember – you can put the horizon at the top or bottom of the shot).

⭐ Try to capture the sunset in a reflection such as a puddle or a shop window.

⭐ Don't forget the clouds! Point a camera into the sky and try to capture the fluffy clouds, as often they will take on an amazing colour too!

Draw and colour the sunset here.

TREASURE HUNT

Do you like to hunt for treasure? How about photographic treasure? If you can believe it, there will be a couple of treasures within walking distance of you right now! Here's a fun photographic treasure hunt that will really put your new skills to the test. Have a go!

TIP!

Remember – the photographs need to be sharp, so make sure you have enough light and you've got your focus square on your subject.

Can you photograph...

* the sole of your shoe?
* the letter T?
* the colour yellow?
* a reflection of you?
* something smelly?
* your shadow?
* something smooth?
* the big sky?
* lines?
* something that is loud?
* happiness?
* blur?
* a black and white image?
* an eye?
* an upside down landscape?
* a splash?
* a star jump?

Can you...

* make a tree look big?
* frame your subject?
* capture a bird in flight?

Ben

Zoe

Mila

Now you've completed this treasure hunt, can you create your own? Ask a family member or friend to complete it with you afterwards for added fun!

1 _____

2 _____

3 _____

4 _____

5 _____

6 _____

7 _____

8 _____

9 _____

10 _____

Hatty

Evie

Dan

ORGANISE

Now that you've taken great photos, spend some time looking through them to choose your favourites. You can organise the photos on a phone, if you've taken them with a phone. If you've taken them with a camera, you can download them to a computer or phone, ready to organise.

Which images would you put in your favourite toy folder?

Jackson

John

Eliana

Create folders for each topic that you've photographed, for example 'Toys', and put your favourite images in them. It's okay if you only have 2 or 3, or if you have 10, that's great too!

Rocco

When you are choosing your favourite photos, consider:

⭐ Is it sharply focused?

⭐ Is it the best example?

⭐ Is it creative?

TIP!

Make sure you choose all your favourites. You can always go back into the favourites folder later and choose fewer.

For the left-over photographs, you can create another folder for each topic. Put the word 'extra' in front of each topic name, such as 'Extra Toys'.

If you do this for all the topics in the book, you'll have a great library of photographs to use for calendars, cards and prints!

Get organising!

EDIT YOUR PHOTOS

Editing is a great way to put the finishing touches on your photographs. You can perfect your photos using an editing program on the computer or an editing app on a phone.

When you edit the photograph, you can make it brighter or darker, crop or get closer to the subject, and even change the colours of the photograph itself. There are so many different ways you can edit a photograph! Try exploring all the editing options to see what makes your photograph look the best.

Start by using an easy or basic editing program to learn more about the editing tools.

3 WAYS TO EDIT YOUR PHOTOS

1 CROP

If you would like to get closer to the subject in the photo, the crop tool will do it!

original image

cropped image

2 BRIGHTNESS

If your image needs more light, try adjusting the brightness. Try moving the tool or lever slowly to see how the image appears brighter and then darker.

original image

edited image

3 SATURATION

If you would like to make the shades of the colours in the photograph brighter, try adjusting the image's saturation levels.

original image

edited image

Now you edit!

Find a photograph that needs to be cropped, and have a go!

Do you have a photograph that is too bright? Try using the brightness tool to make it appear darker.

Look for your favourite colour photograph and saturate it! How does it look now?

PRINT

Try printing out your amazing images so you can display and share your work.

There are several ways to print your images.

1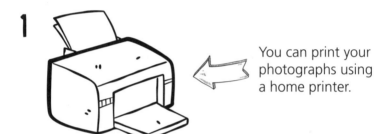

You can print your photographs using a home printer.

2 You can upload your images to a website that will post the printed images to you.

3 You can visit a store or shop that specialises in making photographic prints, and have your photographs printed while you wait.

If you print a photograph at home, try using photographic paper as it will make your image's colours and sharpness stand out. There are lots of paper options – two popular ones are a glossy/shiny paper or a matte/non-shiny paper. The glossy paper looks great with bright colours, and the matte is good for black and white photographs.

How big do you want your image to be? Popular image sizes are 4×6 inches, 5×7 inches, 8×10 inches and A4. Think about how much space you have to display your photos. This can help you decide what size to print.

4×6 inches

A 4×6 inch print is shaped more like a rectangle, which will help to fit in most of your image.

An 8×10 inch print is shaped more like a square, and sometimes can crop out the details on the sides of the image.

8×10 inches

Paper sizes

1 Get a piece of A4 paper, a ruler and a pencil.

2 In the middle of the paper, measure out a 4×6 inch print. Label it 4×6 inches.

3 Now measure out a 5×7 inch print around the 4×6 inch print. Label it 5×7 inches.

4 Measure out an 8×10 inch print, and draw it around the other rectangles. Label it 8×10 inches.

TIP!

The paper you are using is an A4 size – so now you know how large each of your prints could be. This should help you decide on the size for each image.

Get printing!

CREATE

Now that you've printed your favourite images, you can make them into fun gifts.

Try making photo cards with your smaller prints. Find some A4 paper, fold it in half and glue the print on the front of the card. Make sure you put your name or signature either under the print or on the back of the card, as you're the artist!

Postcards are a great way to use your 4×6 inch prints. Get a permanent pen, turn your print over to the plain side and draw a line down the middle of the print. You can now write a message to a friend on the left side and write their address on the right side. Don't forget your stamp!

Make a calendar with your larger prints. You can use an A4 sheet of paper with 5×7 inch prints, or an A3 piece of paper with 8×10 inch prints. Glue the photograph at the top and draw the calendar month below. Think about which photograph will work well with each month. For example, a bright, colourful photo could be paired with a spring month, and a black and white photo would suit a winter month.

Can you think of some more fun ideas for your prints? What about a bug collage or a funny selfie collection?

Zoe

List your own great ideas below.

1 _____

2 _____

3 _____

4 _____

5 _____

Next... go and make them!

SHARE

Sharing your photographs is a wonderful way to show your friends and family your new talent. Your prints, photo cards, calendars and postcards make great gifts for birthdays, Christmas, or just because.

You can personalise your gifts, giving your friends or family members photographs of things they really like. If your friend really likes bugs, think about making a calendar full of bug photos! Or use the letters you've photographed, and try to spell out a friend's name for a birthday present.

Isaac

Another way to share your images is through email or with messenger apps – ask a grown-up to help you. Take an image from your 'favourites' folder and send it with a message to your friend or family member. Sharing your digital files is a way to make someone smile and to share your great work!

Teddy

TIP!

Share a photo a day with a friend or family member who doesn't live nearby. This way you can keep in touch and share your skills!

Amelia

Write 3 friends' or family members' names that are special to you, what they like and the photo to share with them.

Name	What they like	Photo to share

1

2

3

Published by Collins
An imprint of HarperCollins Publishers
Westerhill Road, Bishopbriggs, Glasgow,
G64 2QT

www.harpercollins.co.uk

Text © Lillian Spibey
Photographs © Sharp Shots Photo Club Ltd
All other illustrations © Shutterstock.com

Publisher: Michelle I'Anson
Project manager: Rachel Allegro
Design: Sarah Duxbury
Typesetter: Jouve
Cover: Kevin Robbins

9780008372682

Printed in China

10 9 8 7 6 5 4 3 2 1